RUGBY LAW
explained

A DOWN-TO-EARTH GUIDE TO THE LAWS OF RUGBY UNION

articles from the LEICESTER TIGERS programmes

programmes

expanded and updated

by Mike Mortimer

Forward by Dean Richards

Kairos Press

1996

Copyright © Mike Mortimer 1996

ISBN 1-871344-07-7

First Edition, 1996

Body Text in Oranda BT 10pt.
Imagesetting by CDS Imaging, Leicester.
Cover pre-press by Cavelier Reproductions Limited, Oadby, Leicester.
Printed in Great Britain by Norwood Press, Anstey, Leicester.

British Library Cataloguing in Publication Data.
A catalogue record for this book is available from the British Library.

Cover Picture – Steve Lander refereeing the Pilkington Cup final 1996,
Leicester Tigers v Bath.

Cover photography by Andrew Maw.

Cartoon illustrations by Tony Harding.

Diagrams courtesy of the Rugby Football Union, used by permission.

Kairos Press
552 Bradgate Road
Newtown Linford
Leicester LE6 0HB

CONTENTS

FOREWORD
BY DEAN RICHARDS
OF LEICESTER TIGERS & ENGLAND

When asked by Mike Mortimer to write a foreword for his book, 'Rugby Law Explained', I had little hesitation for two reasons.

In the first instance, all of these articles were written by Mike for the Leicester Tigers Official Programmes, over the 1994/95 and 1995/96 seasons. I, like all of the players, am very proud of our club programme, and are grateful to the team of contributors, under the editorship of Stuart Farmer, for the way they produce such a quality product. We are particu-

larly proud now, as it has been declared 'Club **Programme** of the **Year**' for 1995/96. This award was made following a survey throughout the UK by the Rugby Memorabilia Society, who in their report wrote, "We were terribly impressed with the Leicester programme as it was near perfect". Thanks and congratulations are due to the editor, contributors, and the whole production team.

Secondly, I along with many of the players, have regularly read Mike's articles and have picked up one or two interesting little snippets of information that we otherwise would not have known.

I would not claim to be a studier of the Laws of the game, but I believe that any player, or indeed captain, wishing to maximise his effectiveness on the field-of-play, needs to have a very good understanding. I have also found it most beneficial to find out which laws the referees have recently been instructed to enforce more strictly, or apply differently. Knowing the latest interpretation is vital, especially in situations such as the tackle for instance, where the RFU instructions to the referees changed three times within the last season. Knowing what the referees are expecting of the players, and so avoiding giving away those silly penalty points, is an obvious advantage when playing high profile league, cup, and international rugby.

This book has covered some of the most complex law situations in a way that is accurate and up-to-date, and can be easily understood even by those who have never played the game. This is probably due to Mike's unique background, being one of the very few people who has both played and refereed the game to a very high standard.

In the 70s Mike played over 100 games in the front row for Leicester, where I am told he spent much of his time experimenting on how to 'bend' the laws to suit his own uncompromising style of play. Then after a brief spell playing local rugby, he joined the Leicestershire Society of Referees in the 80s, where he rapidly rose through the ranks to command the respect of the players and clubs as a firm but fair arbiter of the Law. It is difficult to resist using the old adage, 'poacher turned game-keeper', when referring to Mike as a referee.

I found 'Rugby Law Explained' very interesting. It covers most aspects of the game, and can be used as a reference book, or for light easy reading.

I enjoyed reading it – I hope you do.

Dean Richards, Leicester, 1996

FORMING A SCRUM

The place for a scrummage is usually where the infringement or stoppage occurred, unless that place is inside the in-goal area, or near to a goal-line or a touch line. If in the in-goal area, the scrum should be formed five metres out from the goal-line opposite the place of the infringement, and if less than five metres from a touch line, brought in from the touch line to the five metre line. For infringements that happen close to a goal-line the scrummage should be formed so that the feet of the front row and second row players of the defending team are in the field of play (that is, not in the in-goal area). This law has been ammended for 1996/97. All defending players must now have their feet in the field of play.

The scrum should be formed without any intentional delay. Each front row must consist of no more and no less than three players. Two locks must form the second row, and those five players must remain bound to each other and onto the scrum, until it ends. There used to be no maximum number of players that were allowed to form a scrum, others being allowed to join by binding along side the second row, or by forming a third, or even a fourth row!!! However, the convention for eight players from each side to form a scrum has been enshrined in law for the 1996/97 season. (see page 9).

Before the two front rows engage they must be standing not more than an arm's length apart, and the ball should be in the hands of the scrum-half, ready to be put in. The front rows should then crouch so that when they meet, each player's head and shoulders are no lower than his hips, and no player's head is next to the head of a team mate. The loosehead (No. 1) prop binds to the left of his own hooker and the tighthead (No. 3) prop binds to his right. As the players engage in a scrum the loosehead prop places his head on the outside (to his left) of the opposing tighthead, and the tighthead places his head between the opposing hooker and loosehead. The tighthead prop must bind on the opposing loosehead prop by placing his right arm outside the left upper arm of the loosehead and reaching for his body. He is allowed to grip the opposing prop's shirt, but his hand must be more towards the back of his opponent, rather than underneath in the chest area. The loosehead prop may either bind on the tighthead prop by binding his arm inside his opponent's right arm, or place his left hand or forearm on his own left thigh.

Until the ball is put in the hooker must have both feet on the ground, with his weight firmly on one foot and his foremost foot must not be in front of the feet of his props. No player in the front row should do anything which may cause a scrum to collapse. All players in a scrum, other than the front row forwards must bind onto a team-mate's body only, with at least one arm. To be correctly bound these players should use the whole arm, from hand to shoulder, to grasp their team-mate's body at or below the level of his armpit. Simply placing a hand on another player does not constitute proper binding.

Incidentally, the ball is usually put into a scrummage at the loosehead side of the team putting the ball in. This gives the hooker of the attacking side an advantage, as he is closer to the put-in of the ball than the defending hooker.

SAFETY IN THE SCRUMMMAGE

In today's world many professional people in positions of authority, such as teachers, police, doctors etc., run the risk of being sued for damages for actions taken in good faith, while carrying out their jobs. For many years Referee Societies have been most concerned about this, and are fully aware that it could happen to one of their members. NOW IT HAS!

A young 17 year old hooker broke his neck playing for Sutton Coldfield Colts against Burton-upon-Trent Colts in October 1991. As a result he was unfortunately paralysed from the neck down and is seeking more than £1 million in damages from the referee who was in charge of the game. The injury occurred when the scrum collapsed and the injured party is claiming that the referee failed to control the match and exposed the players to unnecessary risk by allowing scrums to collapse repeatedly.

This is the first case of its kind to reach the courts in Britain and could have a devastating effect on the game of Rugby Football, should the judge decide that the referee was negligent. Who is going to volunteer to referee rugby games at school or junior club level, when there is a risk of such action?

All Referee Societies are insured, and the defence of the referee in this case is being backed by the RFU. However the most important message to be gleaned from this sad case is the importance of the introduction of safe practices on the rugby field, and especially when players are scrummaging. The RFU do recognise this and have introduced the 'Rugby Continuum' which is a book of rules that amend the laws of the game to suit the development of young players.

For players of 7 years and under there is no scrummaging and their games are re-started with a free pass, by the non-offending side.

At the age of 8 years the children are introduced to the concept of scrummaging, by the forming of uncontested scrums. Such scrums are made up of one row containing three players from each team, and the side who are awarded the put-in must win the ball. This might seem pointless, but as the scrums are static it allows the referee/coach to ensure that each front row is binding firmly together, all shoulders are above hips, and nothing happens that might cause a scrum to collapse.

When the children reach the age of 10 years the scrums still only have three players from each team, but they are now allowed to push and strike for the ball with a view to gaining possession.

At the age of 12 years, two second row players are added, making a total of five for each team, all other rules being the same as before. Only at the age of 13 years do the teams contain 15 players, with eight a side in the scrummage. This gradual introduction to the techniques and pressures of scrummaging gives the children every chance of establishing their suitability for a position in the front row.

By way of an additional safety measure, all children under the age of 19 have to go through a set routine prior to the engagement of every scrum, and those who are entitled to push may only advance 1.5 metres. Once the packs are formed correctly the referee should insist that the front row players CROUCH then TOUCH their immediate opponent on the shoulder or upper arm, PAUSE in this position until invited to ENGAGE.

This repeated routine of CROUCH-TOUCH-PAUSE-ENGAGE forms good habits so that the players adopt the correct positions, and it also prevents the possibility of one pack charging at the other. Let us hope that all the Youth Development Officers; Pilkington Training Officers; Junior Club Coaches; and school masters are aware of, and are enforcing these safety measures, so that we do not read of another tragic accident.

On 19th April 1996 the young colt who broke his neck while playing for Sutton Coldfield won his case against the referee.

✽ ✽ ✽ ✽ ✽

SAFETY IN THE SCRUMMAGE all starts with the position and binding of the front row forwards. The illustration shows how this should be done.

Points to note:–
1) Backs of both players are flat and not bent.
2) Shoulders are not below the hips.
3) The bind is correct, with neither player pulling downwards.
(Note. Alternative bind for the loosehead prop is shown by the dotted line.)

MIDDLE LINE

SCRUMMAGE UPDATE FOR 1996/97

For the coming season each team must put eight men in the scrummage – no more and no less. Whilst the scrummage is in progress all of these players must remain bound on until the scrum is over. Only on occasions when, for whatever reason, a side is reduced to less than fifteen players may they choose to reduce the number put in the scrummage. On such occasions the opposition may duplicate the move if they wish.

This is an experimental variation introduced in the hope of providing more room for attacking ploys around the perimeter of the scrummage.

It has been common practice over recent seasons for teams to 'drop off' one, or even two of the back-row forwards when defending against an opponent's put-in. Having confidence in the front five's ability to hold the shove, their loose forwards stand on-side, just behind the back foot of the second-row, and form a defensive wall. Backed up by the scrum-half, they have successfully managed to 'snuff out' most opposition moves tried close to the scrum. The new experimental variation on the law is intended to prevent this happening.

Two other minor changes have also been introduced. When a scrummage is ordered close to the goal line it should be moved so that all players in the defending team's scrum have their feet in the field of play, instead of only the front five, as before. Secondly, only the immediate opponent of the player putting the ball in the scrummage has to remain behind the ball when it is in the scrummage. In this way it will now be legal for a scrum-half, having won the ball, to place his foot over it before picking it up to pass – a move that has always gone un-penalised in the past, and is now legal.

THE BALL IN THE SCRUM

When the ball is in the set scrummage the off-side line for those of both sides who are not directly involved, is an imaginary line drawn just behind the feet of the hind most man in the scrum and parallel to the goal-line. Players not involved in the scrum must remain behind this line until the ball is out of the scrum. The players forming the scrum are allowed to break away while the ball is in the scrum, providing they immediately move back towards their own goal-line and also take up a position behind the off-side line as previously described. (see update, p.9)

The player putting the ball into the scrum and his immediate opponent are exceptions to this law, and the path of the ball determines their off-side line. These two players must remain behind and on their own side of the ball. As the ball is moved within the scrum so their off-side line moves accordingly. It is the additional freedom of movement afforded to these players that poses the biggest threat to the side who have won possession of the ball. They are allowed to advance down the side of the scrum, just inches behind the ball making life very difficult for the player who tries to pick the ball up.

Scrum halves are only allowed to advance in this way on the side that the ball was put in. For this reason the forwards usually channel the ball diagonally across the scrum so that it comes to rest just to the right hand side of the number 8. In this way they give the ball the maximum protection from the oppos-

ing predatory scrum-half. Remembering that this player must remain behind the ball it makes it impossible for him to get around the body and legs of the No.8 and stay on-side.

While the ball lies in this position between the right leg of the No.8 and the left leg of the wing forward the referee will rule that it is still in the scrum, but at the same time he will not penalise a player of the side in possession if they choose to play the ball. – 'a clear case of having one's cake and eating it as well'. However if a member of the opposing team attempts to play the ball while it is in the same position, he would be penalised for handling the ball while in the scrum.

Such positive discrimination allowed to the side in possession greatly improves its chances of getting the ball away cleanly. While enjoying the obvious benefits of having the ball in such a position, where it is judged to be either in or out of the scrum, depending on their actions they still have to be careful, because the very second that a member of their team places a hand on the ball the scrum will be judged to have ended. This would mean that all previously defined off-side lines would disappear and the opposition players could advance. Should the scrum-half place his hand on the ball and then change his mind, withdrawing without the ball, he should be penalised for handling in the scrum.

1 METRE

MIDDLE LINE

OFF-SIDE LINE

FORMING A LINE-OUT

The place for a throw-in is indicated by the touch judge and is called the "line of touch". Each team must line up at least half a metre on its side of the line of touch, so as to leave a clear space of one metre between the two lines of players. The players in the line-out must stand between the five metre line and the fifteen metre line. Any player who is further than fifteen metres from the touch line when the line-out begins is not in the line-out.

At least two players from each team are required to form a line out and the maximum number is determined by the team who have the right to throw the ball in. The conventional number of players in a line-out is seven, but if the team throwing in the ball choose to reduce the number then the opposition must also. Failure to do so would entitle the side throwing in the ball to have a free-kick awarded on the line of touch, fifteen metres in from touch. The ball is usually thrown in by the hooker and his immediate opponent must remain within five metres of the touchline on his own side of the line of touch. Once the ball has been thrown in five metres the two hookers can then join the lineout.

One other player from each team (usually the scrum-half) is allowed to take up position to receive the ball if it is passed or knocked back from the line-out. All other players are not participating in the line-out and must take up a position at least ten metres back from the line of touch towards their own goal-line.

When the ball is in touch players who approach the line-of-touch must always be presumed to do so for the purpose of forming a line-out. This is a requirement so the team who are not throwing-in the ball have every chance to establish how many players they can place in the line-out and it stops contrived free-kicks. The line-out starts when the ball leaves the hands of the player who is throwing it in.

UPDATE FOR 1996/97

The law used to state that each team must line up at least half a metre on its own side of the line of touch, when forming a lineout. Teams were able to 'step out' of the lineout, towards their own line, therefore widening the gap, a ploy extensively used as players and coaches felt it gave an advantage. However the law-makers have now deleted the two words "at least", which will prevent players from legally doing this in future. The gap will be exactly one metre, all of the time.

In another change, the law previously made it illegal for a player in the lineout to bind onto any other player of his own team before the ball has been touched by a player participating in the lineout. As this has now been omitted, we can logically assume that there is no restriction on binding in this way. Secondly, the writers add that a player should not support a team-mate before that player has jumped for the ball. Again this indicates that it is legal to do so, once he has jumped.

So at last – supporting a jumper in the lineout is legal, according to the law book – not before time, as it has been going on un-penalised for all of twenty years. The referees have been briefed on how to interpret this law: supporting with flat hands, and fingers pointing upwards, above the jumper's waist, should be permitted providing the jumper leaves the ground under his own steam.

SUPPORTING OR LIFTING?

I have studied referees closely for a few years now and the most common weakness in my opinion is the refereeing of support play in the line-out. Whether at International, Senior League or local level – Northern or Southern hemisphere, the inability to spot offenders and the inconsistency of decision making is often quite alarming. No-one has ever admitted it to me, but I am convinced that many senior referees ensure that they award one penalty against each side for a line-out offence within the first four or five line-outs (usually in a non-kickable position) and then just let the players get on with it.

This leads one to ask – what makes the line-out so difficult to referee? – why do so many referees opt out – and why do individual interpretations of the same law vary so much?

We would probably agree that today most referees are able to achieve a one metre gap between the two teams as they line up for a line-out; the problems all begin once the ball is thrown. While a ball is in the air only players in the act of jumping for it are legally allowed to close the gap – all supporting players should stay where they are until the ball has been touched by a player who has jumped for the ball. When jumping for a ball a player must use both hands or his inside arm to catch or deflect the ball and he should not use an opponent, or another player of his own team, as a support.

The actual time that the ball is touched by a player who has jumped is crucial, because it is only after the ball has been touched that the supporting players can move forward. Before this time they cannot legally bind onto the jumping forward, or any other player on either side.

Now in reality it never happens like this, as all of the supporting players are coached to move in as soon as the ball is thrown. This is done by both teams simultaneously within fractions of a second, leaving the referee in a quandary as to which team he should penalise. The result is that the referees nearly always 'opt-out' – unless an over-zealous supporting player crosses the line of touch and blatantly obstructs a player of the opposing team.

The law clearly states that no player should lift any player of his own team, but in my mind this would not be an issue if the previous points made were refereed properly. Referees should stop supporting players closing the gap and binding before the ball has been touched by a jumping player. Once the ball has been touched it will have been deflected and the line-out is over, or else it will have been caught. If the jumping player has caught the ball he will not appreciate being lifted higher. His prime objective will be to return to the relative safety of the ground with the ball!.

Good refereeing in this aspect of the line-out depends on two simple but key issues:-

1) Only a player in the act of jumping for the ball can enter the metre gap before the ball is touched by a player in the line-out.

2) No player can touch or bind on any other player of either side before the ball is touched by a player in the line-out.

However, see the update for new laws, on the previous page.

Also new for 1996/97, a player jumping for the ball may also now use his outside hand to play the ball, providing both of his arms are raised above his head.

IS THE BALL IN TOUCH?

Being rugby football the answer to the question, 'Is the ball in touch?' is not always obvious. The important points to know are that the touch-lines are in touch and the ball is in touch under the following circumsta nces:

"When it *is carried* by a player and it, or the player, touches a touch-line or the ground beyond it."

"When it is *not carried* by a player and it touches the touch-line or the ground beyond it."

Usually, when the touch judge raises his flag a ball carrier has been bundled into touch by an opponent's tackle, or the ball has been kicked into the back row of the stand. Either way there is little doubt that the ball should rightly be judged to be in touch, but following are four situations to make you think; if you were the touch judge would you raise your flag?

1) A player starting with both feet well in the field-of-play jumps upwards and outwards, beyond the plane of the touch-line and knocks the ball (that was in the air several feet beyond the plane of the touch-line) back into play, before he came to ground.

2) The ball is kicked into the air and travels several yards beyond the plane of the touch-line. While still in the air it is 'picked-up' by a very strong cross wind and blown back into the field of play, where it first bounces.

3) A player who is lying on the ground with both of his legs in touch, reaches out with his hand and taps the ball back towards a player of his own team. The ball was positioned two feet in from the touch-line at the time it was tapped.

4) A player standing with one foot in touch kicks the ball (which is lying well within the field of play) with his other foot.

Those of you that have judged that the ball was not in touch on all of the above occasions may congratulate yourselves as you are correct for the following reasons:

1) The player jumped from within the field of play and did not make contact with the ground until after he had played the ball. Also the ball did not make contact with the touch line or the ground beyond it.

2) The ball never touched the touch-line or the ground beyond it.

3) & 4) Although on both occasions the player was in touch, he did not attempt to *carry* the ball and the ball never touched the touch-line or the ground beyond it.

So, if it is possible for a player to legally play the ball when he has part of his body in touch, providing he does not carry it, and as one only needs to apply downward pressure on the ball to score a try, the following conundrum is posed. Can a player who has his feet in touch score a legitimate try? What are your thoughts?

See page 26 for the correct answer

OFFSIDE IN THE LINEOUT

The line-out is formed by each team lining up half a metre on each side of an imaginary line at right angles to the touch line, and indicated by the touch judge. Each team must have at least two players in the line-out, and the maximum is determined by the side who have the right to throw the ball in.

For the forwards standing in the line, both scrum halves, the player throwing the ball in, and his opposite number, the off-side line is the line-of-touch, until the ball touches a player, or the ground. After that the off-side line runs through the ball itself. So the players taking part in the line-out should stay on their own side of the line-of-touch until the ball arrives, and then they should remain behind the ball until the line-out ends.

The player throwing the ball should stand in touch while making the throw. Once the ball is thrown he can take up a position in the field of play, so long as he remains behind the line of touch, which is the off-side line. His opposite number is the only other forward allowed to stand between the 5 metre line and the touch line, and he too must remain behind the off-side line. The other forwards who are forming the line should not take up a position beyond the 15 metre line, unless the ball is thrown directly to them, otherwise they would be offside.

All players not taking part in the line-out (usually the three-quarters) must take up positions behind the imaginary line at right angles to the touch line, and 10 metres back from the line-of-touch. Should the line-out be awarded nearer than 10 metres to one team's goal-line, the goal-line becomes their off-side line. These players should not advance in front of the off-side line until the line-out is over. So when is the line-out over?

A line-out starts when the ball leaves the hands of the player throwing in, and it ends in one of the five following ways:
1) The ball is passed or tapped out of the line-out;
2) A ball carrier runs out of the line-out;
3) The ball travels beyond the 15 metre line;
4) A ruck or maul forms and the back feet of one team moves beyond the line-of-touch;
5) The ball becomes unplayable and the referee blows the whistle.

Knowing the above law is very important, because while the line-out is still in progress the two sets of backs are usually at least 20 metres apart. It is probably the only time in the game that the backs are assured of this amount of space and time to work in. That is why the better coaches and players spend a lot of time developing the two handed catch in the line-out. When ball is secured in this way the line-out is not immediately over and the opposing backs are not allowed to advance.

The penalty for being off-side in a lineout is a penalty kick, and as they are always awarded at least 15 metres in from the touch line they frequently result in a three point goal.

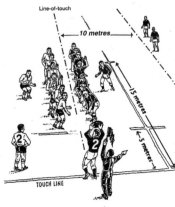

THE QUICK THROW IN

Players have been allowed to take a throw-in quickly, without waiting for a line-out to form, for many years, but such a throw had to be taken from the line of touch exactly where the ball had crossed the touch-line. In an attempt to make the game more exciting and reduce the amount of stoppage time, the RFU introduced a new law in 1992 allowing players to take a quick throw-in from anywhere on the touch-line between the place where the ball went into touch and their own goal-line. This offered the side with the right to throw-in additional attacking options, but they could only take advantage provided they complied with other conditions.

A quick throw-in is not allowed if the line-out has already been formed. (One is deemed to have been formed when two or more players from each side are lined up on either side of the line of touch, in readiness for the throw-in to take place.)

The ball that went into touch is the only ball that can be used for a quick throw-in, and that ball must not have been touched by anyone else except the player taking the throw. If a replacement ball is used, or the quick throw-in taken after a line-out is formed, then the quick throw-in is disallowed and the same team would throw-in back at the line-out, as indicated by the touch judge.

When taking a quick throw-in, the ball, as for a normal line-out, must be thrown in straight so that it travels at least five metres before it touches the ground, or another player. Failure to comply with these conditions would mean that the quick throw-in would be disallowed, and the opposing team given the choice of either a throw-in at the place where the throw-in was attempted, or a scrum 15 metres in on the same line.

The place where a player might attempt a quick throw-in, and the place where a line-out should be formed, could be 50 metres or more apart, making life very difficult for the referee. For this reason, the RFU have asked touch judges to assist by not raising their non-flag carrying arm, to indicate who should throw-in, until after the right to take a quick throw-in has gone. In this way the referee can tell, with a quick glance at his touch judge, whether a quickly taken throw-in was legal or otherwise.

I believe the quick throw-in law, as introduced in 1992, is popular with players, coaches, referees and spectators, so perhaps the law makers are not so far out of touch after all!

By the way, it is possible for a player to throw the ball in quickly to himself, providing the throw-in is straight, and travels at least five metres before it touches the ground.

UPDATE FOR 1996/97

Quick throw-ins have been allowed for three years, provided the same ball is used, and only the player throwing in has touched it. It was therefore thought by most referees that a quick throw-in should never be allowed when a ball carrier has been forced into touch since the tackled player and the thrower must both have handled the ball in touch. Nothing changes these facts, but the law now clearly states that referees are to allow a quick throw-in to take place, even if a ball carrier has been forced into touch.

THE TACKLE

A tackle occurs when the player carrying the ball is held by an opponent and either is brought to the ground or the ball he is carrying comes into contact with the ground. He is deemed to have been brought to the ground if he is on one knee, both knees, sitting on the field of play, or is on top of another player who is on the ground. A ball carrier who is held by an opponent but remains on his feet, is NOT deemed to have bee n tackled, NOR is he tackled if he has been knocked to the ground and is not being held.

Following a tackle the ball carrier may take a number of options, but whichever one is chosen must be actioned immediately. The tackled player may pass the ball, release the ball, or get up and move away from the ball. The requirement to release the ball allows the player to put the ball on the ground, or even to push it along the ground in any direction except forward. The interpretation of "immediately" is very much at the discretion of the referee, but the law makers are very keen to see the ball kept alive following a tackle.

Conversely, the player who executes the tackle must do nothing which prevents the tackled player from playing the ball, and all referees are instructed to referee this point very strictly. Once the ball has been played in this way, none of the players on the ground may interfere with the ball, or attempt to tackle an opponent who picks up the ball. In effect they are out of the game until they get back onto their feet.

Players not involved in the tackle may play the ball on arrival providing they stay on their feet. If individuals who are on the ground have played according to the law, the ball should be available for the first player arriving to pick it up. If it is not then he must resist the temptation of going to ground or he will be penalised. Alternatively, if he remains on his feet and the players on the ground prevent him from picking it up, it is they who will be penalised. On occasions where players from both sides arrive at the same time, and they engage with the ball still on the ground between them, a ruck is deemed to have been formed.

It is very important that the referee applies the law strictly after a tackle and that the first offender is the one that is penalised. Often, potentially good games of rugby are ruined because the ball is not recycled after the tackle, resulting in a pile-up of players and the inevitable scrummage or penalty.

Referees should concentrate on the following points:

1) Ensure the tackler allows the ball carrier to play or release the ball
2) Ensure that the tackled player exercises one of his options quickly
3) Ensure that the arriving players stay on their feet, and do not deliberately dive onto or over the ball
4) Always be sure to penalise the FIRST offender!

UPDATE 1996/97 – So keen are the RFU to keep the ball alive after a tackle, they have amended the law yet again. Now any player who tackles an opponent and, in doing so, goes to ground, must immediately release the tackled player and get up or move away from the tackled player and the ball. He must not play the ball until he is on his feet. Previously it was not clear that this was the case, being left to the interpretation of the referee. It is certainly clear now, and referees are instructed to penalise offenders.

RUCK & MAUL SINCE 1994

My brief is to explain and simplify some of the more complex laws of our game, but as recent seasons have seen the introduction of a series of new laws and amendments it is worthwhile looking at some of the more significant changes that have been introduced.

In the 1993/94 season players were told that they could only join a maul by binding on the player of their team who was at the back of the maul. This was very good as it made it very easy for the referee to spot the negative players who were trying to slide down the sides of a maul. It also made it much easier to keep possession by moving the ball to the back, where opponents could not possibly, legally, get their hands on it.

Players and coaches (not least Leicester) were very quick to realise this, and we saw the introduction of prolonged mauls, slowly trundling on towards the opponents goal-line. A well drilled pack could keep this up indefinitely as opponents could not get near the ball, nor do anything that may cause the maul to collapse. A 20 minute rolling maul, no matter how well executed is not what the law makers intended and so new amendments were introduced in the 1994/95 season, designed to stop this trend and improve the chances of a ball being passed out to the likes of Rory Underwood.

The new law stated that when a maul becomes stationary, or the ball in a maul becomes unplayable a scrum shall be awarded to the side who were NOT in possession when the maul began. When a maul becomes stationary the referees have been asked to say "use it or lose it!" – referring to the ball of course. The side in possession will be given reasonable time for the ball to emerge.

There is an exception to this which states that if a player catches the ball direct from a kick by an opponent (other than from a kick-off or a drop out) and is immediately held by an opponent so that a maul is formed, his team will put in the ball at the ensuing scrummage. The amendment is the clause in brackets, introduced as it was thought that the old law was unfair to the teams who had perfected the art of kicking off or dropping out well.

It is interesting to note that unlike the maul, if the ball in a ruck becomes unplayable, a scrum will be awarded to the side who were moving forward immediately prior to the formation of the ruck. Now it is legally possible to turn a maul into a ruck by simply placing the ball on the floor, or the ball carrier (on his own) going to ground. This will probably result in players deliberately creating rucks as the maul begins to lose momentum.

UPDATE FOR 1996/97

As a further amendment to these laws, the scrum-half must not now take any action whilst the ball is in the ruck or maul, to imply to his opponent that the ball is out. Previously scrum-halves were permitted to throw a dummy pass, or make a dummy run, either to wrong foot their opponents, or more likely to tempt them to advance to an off-side position and give away a penalty kick.

This brings the ruck and maul law in line with the scrummage, where the scrum-halves have not been permitted to dummy since 1994.

FROM RUCK TO MAUL

There is NO WAY in which a ruck can be changed into a maul legally. Quite surprising really as the highest ranking referees allow it to happen week after week. I don't think I have seen a single first-class game this season (including internationals) when it has not been allowed.

As the ball appears at the back of a ruck it can be picked out by a player standing in the scrum-half position, providing he does not burrow in too far. This player then has the option of passing, kicking or running with the ball. The referee will be reasonably sympathetic to the player reaching into the ruck for the ball, but once he places his hands on it the ball is deemed to be out and the off-side lines change immediately. The ball can also be picked up by a player who is bound on at the back of a ruck, providing that he completely detaches himself from the ruck as soon as he has it in his hands. He then has the same options as the player standing in the conventional scrum-half position – he can pass, kick or run with the ball.

What he cannot do is to pick up the ball that is lying at his feet while still maintaining upper body and shoulder contact with his own team mates – and then, without ever having lost contact, tuck the ball under one arm and bind on again with his other arm, thus starting a rolling maul. When this happens the players of the same team as the ball carrier should be penalised for being off-side and obstructing, or else the ball carrier penalised for handling the ball in the ruck. Either way it should always result in a penalty kick to the non-offending side.

This practice is most unfair and is becoming increasingly popular with the players as it continues to go on unrecognised by the referees.

RUCKING OR OBSTRUCTING

The purpose of a ruck is to give both teams an opportunity to win possession of the ball when it has gone to the ground and open play has ended. The All Blacks were the first team to show a clear preference for leaving the ball on the ground and rucking rather than to pick it up. This they believed provided them with quicker and cleaner ball, thanks to the fitness speed and power of their pack. Once the ball was placed on the ground five or six forwards would sweep over the ball like a big black blanket, pushing the opposition back and leaving the ball for the scrum half, like a cherry on a plate. This tactic was so successful that it was soon adopted by most other rugby playing nations.

While the rucking players were engaging with their opponents close to the ball and they were all bound on to one another, this was good fair rugby, but unfortunately teams began to stretch the letter of the law to the limit, and many unfair practices were coached. One such practice became known as 'Scatter Rucking', when instead of focusing at the point where the ball was put on the floor and binding to one another as they arrived the players deliberately spread themselves over a wide area – some three or four metres on either side of the ball – and charge in with their arms outstretched. This charge would continue way past the point where the ball was on the floor, and consequently these forwards would sweep out all the opposition players anywhere near the ball and prevent those behind the ball from getting to the point where the ruck should be taking place. I am sure that you will all recognise this practice for the blatant obstruction that it surely is.

Referees are now advised that players may go beyond the ball providing they do not obstruct opponents in the actions they take (e.g. turning their backs to the opposition or 'scatter rucking' with arms outstretched). Rucking players may only engage with the opposition when in close proximity to the ball. They should attempt to step over players on the ground without contact and should be allowed to take one step before engagement – Any engagement with opponents after this second step would be considered obstruction by the referee. When players drive or are driven to the ground in the absence of opposition the referee should recognise that no ruck has therefore been formed and that this is not an infringement of the law.

The secret of good rucking is for the players to arrive at the breakdown early – in numbers – bound on to one another and then hit the area directly behind the ball, which is the target. When this is done well it will clear the opposition players legally and leave the ball for the scrum half to pick up and continue the team's forward momentum.

UPDATE FOR 1996/97: For the coming season the RFU have included a definition of *RUCKING* in the law book, which reads as follows:

"Rucking is the act of a player who is in a ruck using his feet to retrieve or return a ball without contravening law 26" (Foul Play)

This has been done because of their concern for the safety of players on the floor. Further to this the RFU have stated that rucking must be to retrieve or return a ball, therefore players that ruck at one end, while the ball is clearly at the other, should be penalised. Also, boots should not make contact with players. A boot which makes contact with a player's head will always be regarded as intentional.

OFFSIDE AT RUCK & MAUL

As soon as a ruck or maul is formed during a game of rugby the off-side lines are changed immediately for all players of both teams. For this reason, it is absolutely imperative that players, referees and those who wish to understand the game, know exactly what constitutes a ruck or a maul.

In the simplest terms, a ruck is formed when the ball is on the ground and a minimum of two players (one from each side) are on their feet and bound together with the ball between them. This situation usually arises after a ball carrier has been tackled and the supporting player is grabbed by an opponent before he has a chance to pick up the ball. Once the ruck is formed in this way any on-side player can join, and the ball can only be played with the feet.

A maul is formed when the ball carrier is on his feet and held by a minimum of two players (one from each side). In the case of a maul it is important to remember that there must be a player of the ball carrier's side involved – a ball carrier surrounded by four or five opponents might look like a maul, but is simply a joint attempt to tackle, or dispossess the ball carrier. As with a ruck any on-side player can join a maul.

Following a scrummage, ruck, maul or line-out all players on the side without possession are put on-side as soon as an opponent runs five metres with the ball, or kicks the ball, regardless of their position relative to the ball. Therefore in open play, when the ball is being run and passed between players, only those in the side in possession can be off-side, BUT this changes with the formation of a ruck or maul.

As soon as we have a ruck or a maul two clear cut imaginary off-side lines are introduced immediately. These off-side lines run across the field parallel to the goal lines through the back foot of the hindmost player in each side of the ruck or maul. All players who are in front of their respective off-side line are themselves off-side, and cannot take part in the game until they retire to an on-side position behind the line.

Players wishing to join the ruck or maul must approach from an on-side position and bind to the hindmost player of their own team. They cannot join on to the side of the ruck or maul, nor can they loosen their bind and slide down the sides. Players can leave a ruck or maul at any time, but if they do they must immediately retire to an on-side position behind the back foot of the hindmost player who is in the ruck or maul.

All players who do not join the ruck or maul must remain behind their respective off-side line at all times until the ruck or maul is over. In the case of a maul this often means that players have to retreat if the opponents get a drive on.

Referees should be very strict and penalise any forwards who loiter at the sides of rucks and mauls and backs who encroach beyond their off-side line.

KNOCK-ON AND FORWARD PASS

A knock-on occurs when a player loses possession of, or propels the ball with his hands or arm towards his opponents' dead ball line, and it then touches the ground or another player before it is recovered by that player. If the ball is knocked forward one or more times by a player who is in the act of catching it, and it is recovered by that player before it has touched the ground or another player, then it is deemed to be an adjustment and not a knock-on.

For an unintentional knock-on a scrummage will be awarded, usually at the place of infringement, with the put-in to the non-offending team. It is an offence to intentionally knock-on, and in 1992 the penalty for this was changed from a penalty-kick to a free-kick. However, if the referee decided that a try would probably have been scored had a player not deliberately knocked the ball forward, he can still award a penalty try.

A knock-on can occur anywhere in the playing area, which includes the field of play, and the two in-goal areas. For a knock-on by either team that happens in an in-goal area, the referee should award the scrum to the non-offending side, in the field of play five metres from the goal-line, and in line with the infringement.

As usual, the referee will look to see if the non-offending team can gain an advantage after a knock-on, but there is one occasion when such an advantage is not allowed. If an attacking player knocks the ball forward in the field of play and the ball travels into the in-goal area where it is then grounded by a player, or goes into touch-in-goal, or over the dead-ball-line, a scrummage will be awarded at the place of the knock-on. This is done because the law makers believe that to allow the defending team to gain a 22 metre drop-out from this situation, simply by touching the ball down, is far too great an advantage in view of the fact that their opponents were threatening to score a try.

A knock-on occurs when the ball is propelled forward from a player's hands or arms. It is not a knock-on if the ball is headed forward (soccer style). This was a ploy that was regularly used by Robin Money, who played full-back for Leicester in the 1970s.

Any on-side player is allowed to pass the ball, or propel it with his hand, providing that it does not travel towards his opponent's goal-line. A flat pass or a pass parallel to the goal-line is therefore perfectly acceptable and referees are advised to allow play to continue unless they are sure that the pass was forward. If a pass is not thrown forward, but bounces forward after hitting the ground or another player, the referee should again allow play to continue.

When a player hands the ball to another player of his own team without any propulsion, or throwing of the ball, this also constitutes a pass. Therefore, if the receiving player is in front of the player handing him the ball the pass should be judged to be forward.

It should be noted that the one time that a player is allowed to knock the ball forward without penalty is when the ball is charged down from an opponent's kick. For this to be legal the player should make no attempt to catch the ball, but simply charge forward with his hands and arms outstretched with a view to stopping the kick being made.

UPDATE FOR 1996/97

As mentioned in the previous article, prior to 1992 the penalty for deliberately knocking the ball forward was a penalty kick at the place of the offence. Many people were surprised and could not understand why the penalty was reduced to a free-kick, especially when the referees were instructed that they still had the option of awarding a penalty try should they think the non-offending side probably would have scored a try had it not been for the knock-on offence.

However sense has prevailed, and this decision, which only lasted four years, has been reversed for the 1996/97 season. The penalty for a deliberate knock-on is now a penalty kick to the non-offending side.

KICK-OFFS

The game starts with a kick-off at the beginning of each half and at resumption of play after a team has scored. The kick should be taken from the centre of the halfway line, although most referees will allow it to be taken a yard or two to one or the other side in order to find firm ground or preserve the pitch.

The first kick of each half must be a place kick. Which team kicks-off each half is decided by the toss of a coin before the game starts.

When the game re-starts after a team has scored, a drop kick must be used. This kick should be taken at or behind the centre of the half way line, by the non-scoring team.

For all kick-offs the players on the kicker's side must remain behind the ball until it has been kicked. Players should be particularly careful in the case of a drop-kick, as the kicker may choose to kick from a distance behind the actual half-way line. Failure to keep behind the ball until it has been kicked would result in a scrummage on the half-way line, with the put-in going to the non-offending team.

All types of kick-off must reach the line which is ten metres ahead of the half-way line, unless first played by an opponent. The players waiting to receive a kick-off should be behind this ten metre line until the ball has been kicked. If they move into this ten metre area and there play the ball, they must accept all of the consequences and the game will be allowed to continue. On occasions when the ball does not reach the ten metre line and is not played by an opponent, the game will re-start with the kick taken again, or a scrum mage to the receiving team on the halfway line. The receiving team are asked to make the choice. If, when kicked off the ball crosses

the plane of the ten metre line and is then blown back by a strong wind, play should be allowed to continue.

Should a kick-off be kicked directly into touch without touching the ground or a player, the receiving team then have the following options:

1) Accept the kick
2) Have the kick-off re-taken
3) Have the put-in at a scrummage on the half-way line.

Option 1 is rarely taken, but if the kick was accepted the resulting line-out would be back at the half-way line because the kicker was not inside his 22 metre area and kicked directly into touch. I have not yet seen a team take a quick throw-in from this situation, which would be perfectly legal. In order to take a quick throw-in, the same ball as that kicked into touch must be used and it should only be handled by one player, who then throws it in so that it travels further than 5 metres at right angles to the touch line. The fact that this has not been done is probably just as well, as the option to accept the kick and take the line-out is so rarely taken that it would confuse everyone – referee included.

When the ball from a kick-off crosses the opposing team's goal-line without touching or being touched by a player, the receiving team has the option of grounding the ball and making it dead or playing on. If the ball is grounded and made dead the game would restart with another kick-off, or a scrummage on the halfway line.

For all kick-offs the ball must be kicked from the correct place and by the correct form of kick otherwise it shall be kicked-off again, no advantage applies.

OFF-SIDE IN GENERAL PLAY

This article attempts to simplify off-side when the ball is being passed, run with or kicked by a player in what is known as general open play. It does NOT apply to rucks, mauls, scrums, or line-outs when the off-side laws are different.

In general play a player is off-side if the ball has been kicked, deliberately touched, or is being carried by one of his own team behind him. The off-side line is an imaginary line drawn parallel to the goal lines through the point where the ball was last played or is being held by a player. All players on the same team who are in front of this imaginary line are off-side. Contrary to many people's understanding, off-side law applies from dead ball line to dead ball line and therefore a player can be off-side in his own in-goal area.

It is important to realise that being off-side in itself is not a penalty offence, it simply means that you are out of the game. An off-side player is only penalised if he plays the ball, obstructs an opponent, or moves towards the opponents waiting to play the ball, before he is put on-side.

An off-side player should be looking to get himself on-side and therefore back in the game. He can do this by running back behind the imaginary off-side line himself or waiting for team mates to advance the off-side line. This can be done by the player who last played the ball or any other player who was on-side at that time running forward. The imaginary off-side line will advance at the rate of the fastest on-side player.

Off-side players can also be played on-side by actions taken by their opponents. Once an opponent gathers the ball and runs five metres, kicks or passes the ball all players on the other side become on-side immediately. However, it would not be rugby if we did not have an exception to the rule! When the ball is kicked forward up field, any off-side player who is within a 10 metre radius circle of an opponent waiting to play the ball or of the place where the ball lands, should retire without delay and without interfering with an opponent. No action taken by an opponent will put a player within that circle on-side, and referees are advised to interpret this law strictly. Players are NOT allowed to stand still in this area, they must make the effort to get away.

Players and coaches are looking for strict refereeing of ALL off-side law because the players who are allowed to encroach off-side are negative and unfairly stifle good, flowing, open rugby!

UPDATE FOR 1996/97

The off-side law for general open play has not changed at all, but we should see a more efficient application of it by referees at the highest levels in the future. The RFU have recognised that off-side has become prevalent, and in view of the complexity of these laws, coupled with the increasing speed of players, it is now an impossible task for one official. For this reason, all referees officiating in division one games will in future be 'wired up' with their two touch judges, by two-way radio. This will effectively add two extra pairs of eyes to the task.

The main objective of this is to eliminate foul play, and keep the players on-side, giving the side in possession their legal space in which to work.

More details on the new radio proposals are given on page 55.

THE TRY

The main objective of playing rugby football is to gain more points than the opposing team, by scoring drop goals, penalty goals, tries and conversions.

Drop goals and penalty goals carry a value of 3 points, a conversion 2 points and a try is worth 5 points. There will be those amongst you who can remember the days when a try was only worth 3 points. It has been revalued upwards twice during my playing days, with the intention of encouraging teams to play a more positive passing and running game resulting in the scoring of more tries.

An on-side player can score a try by carrying or kicking the ball over the opponent's goal-line into the in-goal area and then being the first player to touch it down. Touching down requires the player to place downward pressure onto the grounded ball with the hands, arms or upper body (from waist to neck inclusive). The ball should be under the control of the player carrying it, or lying on the ground at the time it was touched down. The pressure applied must be downward-Picking up the ball is not grounding it.

The goal-line is in the in-goal area and therefore a try should be awarded if the attacking player places downward pressure on the ball whilst it is on the line. The goal posts, which are set into the goal line, are also in the in-goal area and a try should be awarded if the ball is touched down while it is in contact with the ground and the base of the post.

On the other hand, the corner posts are in touch in-goal and therefore if one is touched by the ball carrier before he is able to ground the ball in the in-goal area, a try should not be awarded. The game would be restarted with a 22 metre drop-out to the defending side.

If a ball carrier is tackled and the momentum of the player carries him in to the opponents in-goal and he then touches the ball down, a try should be awarded. What one cannot do is to propel the body further forward in order to reach the line, by using the arms or legs in a second action. However a player who has been tackled short of the line, but is in such a position that he is able to ground the ball on or over the line, without propelling his body forward a second time, should be allowed to do so. Provided a try is scored by the second placement of the ball this is legal. This is an exception to the very strict tackle laws and a further exception is that this is the only time that a tackler can legally try to stop the tackled player playing the ball. Although this law is quite clear, many senior referees do not allow tries to be scored in this way.

When there is doubt as to which team first grounded the ball in the in-goal, a scrummage should be formed five metres from the goal-line opposite the place where the ball was grounded. This also applies when a player is held up in the in-goal area and unable to ground the ball.

A penalty try is awarded on occasions when in the opinion of the referee a try would probably have been scored − or scored in a more favourable position, had it not been for foul play on the part of the opposition.

Answer to question on page 14

A player who has his feet in touch can score a try by placing downward pressure on a ball that is lying in the goal area. Only if he picks the ball up is it deemed to be in touch.

PENALTY TRY FOR REPEATED INFRINGEMENT?

During the 1995 Varsity match the referee, Mr Tony Spreadbury, awarded a penalty try to Cambridge for repeated infringement by Oxford, who were the defending side. This being the first such decision in a high profile game it instigated quite a lot of debate, with many of the learned members of the press concluding that such a decision was not supported by the laws of the game – how wrong they were!

The law states that *"a Penalty-try should be awarded if, but for foul play by the defending team, a try would probably have been scored."* Foul play is covered by law 26 which states – *"Foul play is any action by a player which is contrary to the letter and spirit of the game, and includes obstruction, unfair play, misconduct, dangerous play, unsporting behaviour, retaliation and repeated infringements."*

This section in law dealing with repeated infringements is most commonly applied to scrum-halves and hookers who either put the ball in the scrum, or throw it in at the line-out not straight. Most referee societies would agree that three consecutive, wilful offences of the above, would constitute repeated infringement and a penalty kick would be awarded to the non-offending team.

The Varsity match was different because Oxford, who were defending their own goal-line, were repeatedly standing in front of the off-side line and closing down the space that Cambridge should have had to work in. Most referees would play advantage and if non occurred then award another penalty kick, which must of course be five metres out from the goal-line. Tony Spreadbury warned Oxford of the possible consequences of wilfully standing off-side and so, when they repeated the infringement, he awarded a penalty try, because in his opinion had it not been for such foul play, Cambridge would probably have scored anyway.

With the introduction of league and cup football there is far more pressure on the teams to win the game. As a result defending players often deliberately kill the ball, or stand off-side, in the knowledge that the penalty kick is only worth 3 points, compared to a possible 5 or 7 for a try. This practice becomes even more prevalent once the attacking team are within 5 metres of the goal-line, because any subsequent penalty kick can only be awarded 5 metres out from the goal-line.

If we want to see a free-flowing, running and passing game then the deliberate and repeated infringements need to be stopped. We need more referees like Tony Spreadbury who has shown that he has the bottle to penalise them and even award a penalty try. Well done Tony Spreadbury!

Members of the press would do well to study the laws of the game that they are handsomely paid to report on.

UPDATE: At the time of writing the above, I was blissfully unaware that a similar decision would deny Leicester Tigers the Pilkington Cup in May 1996. On that occasion the referee was Steve Lander (featured on the front cover, refereeing the same game) who judged that Leicester was guilty of repeated infringement when defending their line during the dying moments of the game. The resulting penalty try and conversion cost Leicester the cup – another very brave decision!

KICK AT GOAL AFTER A TRY

In order to encourage the scoring of more tries, the law gives the successful team the opportunity of scoring an additional two points making the try worth a total of seven points in all. To beat this, an opposing team relying on penalties or drop goals, would have to score three times. The additional two point bonus is awarded if a member of the try-scorer's team is able to kick the ball over the opponent's cross bar and between the goal posts.

The kick must be taken from somewhere on a line through the place where the try was scored and parallel to the touch line. Providing the ball is kicked from this line it can be as close or far away from the goal-line as the kicker chooses. The further back the wider the angle.

The kick should be taken with the ball that was in play when the try was scored and by any member of the try-scoring team. The kicker may use a place kick or a drop-kick. For a place kick an approved kicking tee, sand or another member of the kicker's team may be used to steady the ball. An interesting fact is that if another player is used as a placer of the ball, the ball must remain in contact with the ground at the time it is kicked, whereas modern approved kicking tees and sand stand the ball up at least two inches above the ground – is this fair?

The opposition should all be behind their own goal-line until the kicker begins his run-up. Once the kicker offers to kick the ball they are then allowed to run out in an attempt to charge the kick down. If the opposition charge prematurely and the kicker fails to convert the ball the kick should be taken again, and the offending team ordered not to charge. On occasions when the defending side charge prematurely and the kicker is successful, then that kick should be allowed to stand.

The kicker should not be permitted to be unreasonably slow in taking the kick at goal and a period of one minute between the indication to kick and the actual kick is stated as being well within the zone of 'undue delay'. A player who is unreasonably slow should be warned and if he persists the kick should be disallowed and a kick-off is ordered to the other team. Any time in excess of 40 seconds taken by the kicker would now be added on by the newly appointed RFU timekeepers.

THE MARK OR FAIR CATCH

Ask any fullback and he will confirm that having to wait under a ball that has been kicked skywards by an opponent, with eight burly forwards in chase, is a very un-nerving experience. In order to afford players in such a situation a little additional protection the mark or fair catch was introduced to the laws of the game.

The mark is now very much a defensive play as it can only be claimed from inside a player's twenty two m etre area, or in his in-goal. When executed properly the referee blows his whistle as soon as the word "mark" is shouted and the ball is cought simultaneously. The player who called the mark is then awarded a free-kick on the mark. As with all free kicks, the opposing side have to retire 10 metres giving the player who made the mark, every chance to clear his line.

Up until 1992 the player calling the mark had to be stationary, with both feet on the ground, cleanly catch the ball direct from a kick by an opponent, and at the same time shout "MARK!" This required a little co-ordination, but it was quite surprising how many claimed marks were not awarded because the shout was not clear, or too late.

For the 1992/93 season the law was changed, doing away with the requirement for the player making the mark to be stationary, with both feet on the ground. From that date a fair catch could be awarded to a player who has at least one foot on the ground, cleanly catches the ball, and at the same time exclaims "MARK!" This requires a little less co-ordination, but more importantly can be made by a player while he is on the move – remember he is often being pursued by a band of marauding forwards.

If the ball after being kicked by an attacking player, rebounds off a goal post, or cross bar, it can still be marked by a defending player, providing he complies with the other requirements of the law. Once a mark has been awarded, only the player who claimed it is allowed to take the resulting free-kick. If for some reason that player is unable to do so – maybe through injury – then the game would be restarted with a scrum to the defending team at the place of the mark.

A little known but interesting fact, is that prior to 1992 a player could have claimed a "fair catch" from a ball that was knocked on, or thrown forward by an opponent. The removal of this option, just two years ago, has made very little difference because even with my considerable years of playing and refereeing experience, I have never seen or heard of a player claiming a mark from a knock-on! I might also add, that even if a player did legally claim a mark in this way, the chances of the referee knowing that part of the law, were also pretty slim!

UPDATE FOR 1996-97

The law now requires a player, in his own 22 metres, to cleanly catch the ball and at the same time shout "MARK!" The requirement to have one foot on the ground has been deleted and so it is now possible for a player who has jumped off the ground to make a mark.

Should a player jumping for the ball land outside his 22 metre area, after catching the ball and shouting "MARK!", the mark will be awarded provided the catch itself took place within the 22 metre area.

PENALTY KICKS

The loudest blow on the whistle of the referee usually indicates that he is about to award a penalty kick. Having blown his whistle in this way he should then indicate which side has been awarded the kick, by raising a straight arm, at an angle of 60 degrees to the horizontal, pointing in the direction of the non-offending side. He should then indicate the mark from which the kick is to be taken, followed by a signal to show the reason for the penalty being awarded. On some occasions there may be a choice of two marks and then it is up to the captain of the non-offending side to choose which he prefers. For penalty kicks that are awarded for offences committed when the ball is dead, the referee should make a mark where the ball would next have been in play under normal circumstances. For instance if one hooker prevented his opposite number from throwing the ball in quickly by obstructing him the referee should award a penalty to the non-offending side fifteen metres in on the line-of-touch. When awarded a penalty the non-offending side always have the option of taking a scrummage at the mark instead of a kick.

Having elected to kick the penalty, it can be taken by any member of the non-offending team and by any form of kick with the following provisos:

- If the kicker chooses to hold the ball he must propel the ball out of his hands.
- If the ball is to be placed on the ground the kicker must propel it a visible distance. For this type of "tap kick" the kicker may keep his hand on the ball while he kicks it.
- If the kicker elects to kick for touch

the kick must be a punt or a drop kick.

The kick should be taken on or behind the mark, but not in front or to either side of the mark. A kick taken from the wrong place should be declared void and a scrummage awarded to the other side on the mark. The kick must be taken with the ball that was in play at the time the penalty was awarded, unless the referee decides that the ball is defective. Sand, sawdust or approved kicking tees are legally available for the kicker to place the ball on.

The kicker may play the ball in any direction and he can play the ball again, without any restriction unless he has indicated his intention to kick at goal. Any indication of intention to kick for goal is irrevocable. If the kicker is taking a kick at goal, all players of the opposing team must keep still from the time the kicker commences his run until after the ball has been kicked.

When the penalty offence is within 5 metres of a goal-line the referee should always award the kick five metres out on a line through the mark. A penalty kick should never be awarded closer than five metres from the goal-line. (International referees please note! – IRELAND v ENGLAND January 1995)

Players on the side who have been awarded a penalty should be behind the kicker when the ball is kicked and players of the other side should retire ten metres or to their goal-line to avoid being offside. However, if their failure to be on-side is due to the speed at which the penalty kick was taken, then play should be allowed to continue.

THE QUICKLY TAKEN TAP PENALTY

All penalty- and free-kicks must be taken at or behind the mark as indicated by the referee. If the place of the offence is within five metres of an opponent's goal-line, the mark for the penalty or free-kick should be five metres back from the goal-line. The kick can be taken by any player of the non-offending team and using any form of kick. The kicker may kick the ball in any direction and he may play the ball again without any restriction.

The other players in the kicker's team should be behind the ball until it has been kicked, or else they are deemed off-side. However, retiring players who are in off-side positions will not be penalised if their failure to retire is due to the rapidity with which the kick has been taken, but they must not stop retiring until put on-side by the ball carrier running five metres.

When a penalty or free-kick is awarded all of the players need to know quickly whether they are taking the kick or defending. This has become even more important since 1992 when the law change allowed the kicks to be taken quickly without having to wait for all players to get into on-side positions. The better referees oblige by blowing their whistles a little louder than they would do for a scrum or line-out and at the same time they signal who is to take the kick and where it should be taken from. When done properly this gives the non-offending team the opportunity of gaining advantage by taking the kick quickly if they wish.

Quickly taken penalty or free-kicks are either taken by the player kicking the ball from his hands or else placing it on the ground and tapping it. If the kicker elects to kick the ball while holding it, he must propel it out of his hands and if the ball is placed on the ground, he must propel it a visible distance. For the latter the kicker may keep his hand on the ball while it is kicked along the ground.

The defending team must run without delay to, or behind, an imaginary line parallel to the goal-line and ten metres from the mark, or to their own goal-line if that is nearer. Retiring players will not be penalised if their failure to retire ten metres is due to the rapidity with which the kick has been taken, but they must not stop retiring until an opponent carrying the ball has run five metres. No player of the defending team is allowed to do anything that might stop the non-offending team from taking the kick quickly. This applies to such actions as wilfully carrying, throwing or kicking the ball away out of reach of the kicker. For such actions the referee would advance the mark ten metres.

Referees are very keen to see that the non-offending team get every opportunity of taking the kicks quickly if they wish, but unfortunately this enthusiasm often gets the better of them and many players are taking advantage of this. Even at international level the following infringements are regularly not picked up.

- Scrum-halves are allowed to place the ball on the mark and pick it up and run without any kick.
- Players are being allowed to take the kick to the sides of the mark and very often even in front of the mark
- Kicks are being taken within five metres of the goal-line (this was allowed when Ireland scored against England in 1995)
- When kickers opt to kick the ball from the hand the ball never leaves their hands.

Players wishing to take advantage by kicking a penalty or free-kick quickly, have an obligation to ensure that the ball is properly kicked at a place on or behind the mark. Referees should ensure that this is done.

UPDATE FOR 1996/97

Previously players defending against a quickly taken penalty kick, providing they had been retiring, were put on-side by the ball carrier running five metres. This is no longer the case. Defending players at a penalty must retire and continue to do so, until they have run to a point ten metres away from the mark from which the ball is being kicked.

PLAYERS' DRESS

In November 1994 I was fortunate enough to see Wales play against South Africa in Cardiff, and a fine game it was! However, having seen the dress of many of the South African players, at first hand, I was prompted to write an article on the subject.

Sporting fashion has changed radically in recent times; cricketers have taken to wearing brightly coloured pyjamas, boxers are wearing skirts, soccer clubs seem to be trying to outdo each other with who can wear the most gaudy outfit – while some international rugby players are wearing the oddest fitting shirts manufactured by the very poorest of tailors! (or are they wearing harnesses underneath?)

The International laws of rugby football are very clear and state that a player must not wear any harness or support on any part of his body above the waist. It is permissible to wear thin pads of soft material such as cotton wool or sponge rubber, provided that the pads are either taped to the body or sewn into the jersey. Players are also banned from wearing head guards, with the exception of the Rhino Scrum-Cap which has been approved by the RFU. This stance has been made by the RFU for the following reasons:

• Harnesses and helmets give the wearer a false sense of security which might encourage play in a more dangerous fashion than might otherwise be the case.

• They give the wearer an unfair advantage over the other players.

• They encourage individuals to play whilst injured.

Players are permitted to wear supports on their legs providing they have no rigid reinforcement (shin guards excepted). Referees are asked to look out for illegal supports along with other dangerous projections, such as, buckles, rings and even the odd ear ring! Boot studs also come into this category, but are rarely a problem these days, as most players are aware of which are legal and which are not, and accept that the legal studs are safe.

The referee is entitled to inspect a player's dress at any time, before or during a game, and can insist on the removal of any illegal support or dangerous projection, before that player may resume playing. In the past, most referees (myself included) have chosen not to look too closely at what players are wearing for support on the upper body – but having seen how the southern hemisphere teams are now prepared to present themselves for a game of rugby, one might advise referees to conduct a strip search before every game!

Who knows, such action may even assist the Referee Society's recruitment drive!

UPDATE FOR 1996/97

The law now clearly indicates that players may not wear any of the following:-

• Shoulder pads of the harness type.
• Braces or supports which include any rigid reinforcement.
• Helmets or headguards except RFU approved Rhino and Gilbert.
• Undergarments which include padding.
• Clothing that has become bloodstained during the match.
• gloves.
• Dangerous projections such as buckles or rings.

NEW LAW BULLETIN

Those who watched England win the Grand Slam game against Scotland in March 1995 may remember the moment in the second half when Leicester's Graham Rowntree won his first cap by replacing Jason Leonard. Jason had to leave the field because he had sustained an open wound and as most people are now aware, from the beginning of that season he would be allowed ten minutes to control the bleeding, cover the wound, and report back to the touch judge. Failure to comply within the ten minutes allowed would result in the replacement becoming permanent. Many people suggested at the time that Jason was off the field for longer than ten minutes, and that Graham Rowntree should have remained on the field.

If Jason had been off the field for longer than ten minutes, that would have been the case had it not been for the ruling by the International Rugby Football Board which became law with immediate effect on the day of that match:

"On the advice of the Medical Committee it was decided to remove the restriction on the number of occasions and the length of time that a temporary replacement may be used whilst bleeding wounds are being treated.

"A player who has an open wound must leave the playing area until such time as the bleeding is controlled and the wound is covered or dressed. Such a player may be replaced on a temporary basis, but if unable to resume playing the replacement becomes permanent."

It would appear that on the day in question the referee and the touch judges were applying this new version of the law which was known only to the I.R.F.B. and themselves. I wonder if anyone thought to tell the players and the coaches?

There was another law change in the same bulletin, no doubt inspired by the sending off of John Davies, the Welsh prop forward.

"In the event of a front row forward being sent off, the referee, in the interests of safety, will confer with the captain of his team to determine whether another player is suitably trained/experienced to take his position. If not the captain shall nominate one other forward to leave the field and be replaced by a front row forward.

"This may be done immediately, or if the captain wishes, after he has tried another player in the position.

"Furthermore, where a team has used all its front row forwards the game will continue with non-contested scrums as defined in the Law Variation at Under 19 Level."

MAY I LEAVE THE FIELD SIR?

The playing enclosure embraces the field of play, the in-goal and a reasonable area surrounding it, which can be simply described at a club such as Leicester as the area inside the barriers. During a match only the players, the referee and the touch-judges are allowed in this area without the special permission of the referee.

Before each game the referee would ask each team if they had any medically trained people available and it is possible that suitably trained staff could be given permission to come onto the field to treat injured players while the game is in progress. Without such special permission, granted before the game, other people such as coaches, baggage attendants, doctors and first aid personnel must only come on when summoned by the referee.

Once the game has started the players are not allowed to leave the playing enclosure without the permission of the referee and this even applies during the period of time allotted for half-time. Any player that is permitted to leave the playing enclosure for treatment to an injury or some other special circumstance (I am tempted to tell you the story of a past-president of the Tigers who had to leave the field for a call of nature) must not resume playing until the referee has given

him permission, and this will only be done while the ball is dead.

Any player who wilfully comes back on to the field without the referee's permission in order to assist his team, or obstruct an opponent, could be penalised for misconduct, which comes under 'law 26 – foul play'. If the offence was judged not to be wilful interference but the offending team gained an advantage the referee should order a scrummage to the non-offending team at the place where the player resumed playing without his permission.

In the modern game all sorts of people seem to want to get in on the act and run onto the playing enclosure. We have ball-boys, club mascots, people carrying kicking tees and the water-bottle man. The latter has become such a nuisance that the RFU have issued a new ruling stating that water carriers are not allowed to enter the playing area and must remain beyond the touchline, touch-in-goal-line and dead ball line. The players although still not allowed to leave the playing area to receive water, on medical advice are encouraged to drink water during a match and may meet with the water carriers around the perimeter of the ground for this purpose.

UPDATE FOR 1996/97

The referee must not permit a team, or individual players, to leave the playing area in order to change jerseys unless the jersey has become bloodstained, in which case it *must* be replaced. This is in line with the ruling on open or bleeding wounds and has become law to protect the players from blood-borne viruses such as AIDS or Hepatitis 'B'.

FRONT ROW REPLACEMENTS

It has often been said that to play in the front row of the scrummage one has to be a little mad. It certainly helps, as such players are forced into direct physical contact with their opposite number every time the referee orders a scrummage. When in the scrum they push, shove and wrestle with their opponents and occasionally get to play the ball with their feet. Once the combat of the scrum is over and they are free to run about the field the ball is usually so far away that they rarely receive a pass. Despite all this, they will almost to a man, declare a great love for and pride in their position. This is because of the very special individual and unit skills that they develop, which is enhanced by the comradeship brought about by the fact that they are forced to rely very heavily on each other. Recognition of the front row as a very specialised position has led the RFU to implement special laws for the replacement of front row players.

In the interests of safety every team must have a replacement (or other player on the field) who is capable of playing in the front row, should a replacement be required due to an injury, or even an ordering-off. If a team could not provide a suitable replacement for the front row the referee would order uncontested scrums for the remainder of the match, but under such circumstances, no matter what the score was, the team unable to replace the front row forward would be deemed to have lost the match.

On occasions when a team have used their front row replacement and a second replacement is required, but not available, the referee should again order uncontested scrums, but this time the final score would count.

This applies to the Pilkington Cup, Pilkington Shield, CIS Championship and Courage League games at all levels. For those of you who think that this law will never be called into action – I am reliably informed by the National Referee Development Officer that it already has!

NON-CONTESTABLE SCRUMS

Non-contestable scrums are the same as normal scrums except that:–
- There is no contest for the ball.
- The team putting in the ball must win it.
- Neither team is permitted to push.
- The formation of both teams must be 3-4-1. If one team is one player short, then both scrummages would be 3-4 formation, 3-2-1 if a team is two players short, and 3-2 for an absence of three players.

All of these measures have been introduced with safety in mind. Remember non-contestable scrummaging is only introduced when at least one of the front row players is not a regular front-row forward. In this way, that player is never put under pressure and the scrummage is always equally balanced.

ABANDONED GAMES

Abandoned rugby games are few and far between, but Leicester supporters will recall two incidents of floodlight failure within four matches over the Christmas 1995 period, which might have both resulted in abandoned games.

When Leicester took on Exeter in the fourth round of the Pilkington Cup the floodlights failed in the second half due to a power failure. On this occasion the game had kicked off at 3.00pm and although the light was not good at the time of the floodlight failure, the referee decided that it was safe to continue. It was a very dull and murky day, and being the 23rd of December it was only 2 days past solstice (the shortest day of the year for the Northern hemisphere) and the chances of completing the full 80 minutes was looking doubtful. However this was not put to the test, as the lights were rekindled after a few minutes of play.

More recently, we experienced another floodlight failure at Welford Road, when the first team played Bedford on Friday 19th January. There was no natural light to save the game on this occasion as the match kicked off at 7.15pm. After waiting for 5 or 6 minutes to see if repairs were possible the referee took the only option available to him and abandoned the game.

This game was a friendly – the two sides being in different divisions – and so the final score was of little consequence. However it did pose the question. What should be done if such a thing happened in a league or cup game?

The answer is, as you would expect, clearly covered by the laws of the game. The referee has the power to declare no-side before time has expired if in his opinion the full time cannot be played, or if the continuance of play would be dangerous. If a league game is stopped because of weather conditions or floodlight failure the time of abandonment becomes crucial. If more than 60 minutes of rugby has been played (that is more than 20 minutes of the second half) then the score at the time of the abandonment becomes the match result. If less than 60 minutes has been played then the two teams should play again within 7 days.

The outcome of a game that is stopped for any reason other than weather conditions, will be determined by the organising committee of the league concerned.

BLOODY RULES

As recent as three years ago, when a player took a knock or was cut the decision as to whether he should continue to play or not was based solely on the risks to that individual. On many occasions we have seen pl ayers allowed to continue with blood flowing from wounds that were considered not to be life threatening, or in a dangerous position. Unfortunately we have all now had to adapt our lives in order to take precautions against such deadly viruses as AIDS and Hepatitis 'B', both of which are blood borne.

The first priority of the referee has always been to the safety of the players and as these viruses are transferable from blood to blood, anyone who is bleeding in a contact sport becomes a threat to all of the other players. The laws of rugby football recognise this and state:

"A player who has an open or bleeding wound must leave the playing area until the bleeding is controlled and the wound covered or dressed. Such a player may be replaced on a temporary basis only until the wound is covered or dressed, but after ten minutes the replacement becomes permanent. The ten minute period commences when the player leaves the playing area." The law was amended again at the beginning of this season, and ruled that a player with a bleeding wound may be temporarily replaced only once.

An interesting point is that the ten minute maximum time allowance only comes into operation if a temporary replacement is used. Without the use of a temporary replacement it would appear that an injured player can go off for treatment as many times as he wishes, and for as long as he wants, and still continue playing in the game.

Leicester is a club that has taken the threat of Hepatitis 'B' very seriously and all of the players have been immunised against it. Another noticeable change brought about by the threat of blood borne viruses is the trend for rugby clubs to replace the much lampooned communal bath with showers – whatever next?

This law was amended again in 1995 and the player who goes off to receive treatment for a bleeding wound may take as long as required to stop the bleeding, and then return to the game – the ten minute restriction has been waived.

ADVANTAGE

Until the year 1896 referees were simply used as adjudicators, the captains of the teams had, as in cricket to appeal for a decision. Ironically it was this system which produced the advantage law which most distinguishes rugby football, for no captain would appeal for a stoppage if his team had gained an advantage from an opponents mistake. In 1896 the practice of appeals was done away with and the referee became "the sole arbiter of the law" as stated in the laws as they are today. Referees continued to apply the principle of advantage, established so long ago, by not whistling for an infringement which gains an advantage to the non-offending team.

The law states that *"an advantage must be either territorial, or such possession of the ball as constitutes an obvious tactical advantage. A mere opportunity to gain advantage is not sufficient."* This law places a huge responsibility on the shoulders of a referee, for he alone judges whether an advantage has been gained or not. With the definite exception of foul play, the more artistic referees usually look for reasons NOT to blow their whistles.

However, I have to inform you, if you ever wanted to "stir up a hornet's nest" at a referees meeting just ask for a few opinions on the advantage law! It is the one law in the book that leaves a lot of scope to the interpretation of the individual and overall agreement is rarely achieved. Some of the most contentious aspects of the law being:

1) Is time relevant? How long do the non-offending team have to try and gain an advantage?

2) Should the referee signal that he is playing advantage, or does this give too big an advantage to the non-offending team?

3) Should the referee take into consideration the individual skills of the players on the field? e.g. A goal kicker who can score from the half way line.

4) Should the referee try to play advantage to the defending team when they are in their own 22 metre area?

5) Should the referee vary the amount of advantage he plays, according to the temper of the game?

The referees can't agree on answers to the above, which explains why it is very much an art and not a science, and why there will always be inconsistencies from one referee to another.

A referee is not allowed to play the advantage law under the following circumstances:

1) When the ball or the player carrying it touches the referee – this requires a scrummage to the side in possession.

2) When the ball emerges from either end of the tunnel at a scrummage, not having been played by a front-row forward – re-scrum.

3) When the ball is knocked on by an attacking player, and rolls into the in-goal area where it is then touched down by a defending player – scrum five metres out from the goal line. The defending side gets to put the ball in.

KEEPING THE GAME ALIVE

All rugby enthusiasts are seeking fast free flowing rugby with the ball being carried in the hand and inter-passed between the players, resulting in the scoring of tries. On the frequent occasions when games fall short of this pattern, it can usually be attributed to one of three reasons :-

1) A team decides that its strength is in the pack and the ball is rarely given to the backs, who when they get it are under instructions to kick it back towards their forwards.

2) The players do not comply with the tackle law. The ball carrier does not release the·ball properly – the tackler prevents quick release of the ball – and arriving players do not stay on their feet.

3) The referee is not firm enough at applying the law in the tackle situation, or when he does he is unable to pick out the first offender.

There is little that can be done about the first reason as this is purely in the hands of the players and coaches. It is not a recipe for attractive rugby, but it can win games and the players end up with the game they deserve – pity about the spectators!

However reasons 2) and 3) are to do with the interpretation and application of a specific law which has been under close scrutiny of the RFU law makers over recent seasons. At the beginning of the 1994/95 season all referees were advised that law 18 (the tackle) should be refereed strictly and that the onus should be on the tackling player to allow the ball carrier to either pass, or place the ball as long as it is done immediately. Although this has improved the flow of the game the RFU were still not satisfied and new guidelines were issued. The referees are now asked to inform both captains before each game that the tackled ball carrier must immediately move the ball away from his body. Failure to do this would result in a penalty kick against the tackled player for 'holding the ball' if an on-side, arriving player was not able to pick up the ball easily.

So the priorities for referees on law 18 (the tackle) are now as follows:-

1) make sure the tackled player immediately plays the ball and moves it away from his body.

2) Make sure that the tackler does not prevent the tackled man from playing the ball (stressing that the onus is on the tackler to allow tackled player to play the ball)

3) All other arriving players must stay on their feet .

Lets hope that the RFU have finally come up with the correct formula, and Rory Underwood and his fellow wingers get to see a little more of the ball.

(See also the update to "The Tackle" on page 17)

THE REFEREE

According to the law there should be a referee appointed by the Union for every match, but if there is no appointed referee one can be mutually agreed upon by the two teams. The referee is responsible for keeping the time and the score, and should apply the laws fairly without any variation or omission. He should not give instructions or advice to either team before the kick-off, and during the match should only consult with the two touch judges.

The referee is the sole judge of fact and of law and his decisions are binding on the players. He cannot alter a decision except when given before he observes that a touch judge has raised his flag. During the match, no-one other than the players, the referee and the touch judges are allowed within the playing enclosure unless it is with the permission of the referee. No player should leave the playing enclosure without the referee's permission, and if one does leave the field he must not resume playing in the match until the referee has given his blessing. The players must respect the authority of the referee and must (except in the case of a kick-off) stop playing at once when he has blown his whistle.

Managing a game between thirty players, according to a set of complex laws, has never been an easy task – and made even more difficult by the recent introduction of league and cup competitions. Being fully aware of the responsibility placed on the referees, the Rugby Football Union have installed a structure of county Societies who are responsible for the recruitment, training, grading and appointing of referees within their area. As the standard of rugby varies tremendously between a local club third team and a first division side such as Leicester, the refe-rees are graded nationally within four broad categories. This is done so that a competent referee can be appointed to games of all levels. The grade bands are 'C-List', 'B-List', 'A-List' and 'RFU Panel'.

'C' grade referees cover the vast majority of local junior rugby games. The better referees within this category would be given up to Courage League level 9, which in Leicestershire for example, would include Coalville, Lutterworth, South Leicester and Kibworth. Referees capable of taking more senior games are promoted to level 'B' and would generally referee games between Courage league level 9 and 6. The very best of the 'B' referees are selected on to a 'B1' grade by regional groups and they referee at league levels 4, 5 and 6. It is at this stage that referees begin to travel about the country on exchange, so that they might be observed by RFU assessors. Those 'B' referees who show the potential to make the pinnacle of RFU panel are selected on to the 'A' list, and regularly appointed to referee at Courage league levels 3, 4, 5 and 6.

The RFU Panel might be considered as the 'cream of the crop', as they referee County Championship games and Courage league divisions 1, 2, and 3. Within this category about ten referees are selected for special attention in order to assess their potential at international level. Generally it takes around 8-10 seasons for the most talented of the referees to work their way to the top.

All county Societies are short of referees – so if you think you can do better than the man in the middle, please contact the secretary of your local county society – they will be pleased to welcome you into the fold.

REFEREE SIGNALS

Referees have adopted hand signals as an aid to the communication between themselves, the players and the spectators. The signals come in two basic groups, PRIMARY and SECONDARY.

Primary Signals relate to the award the referee has made to the non-offending side and their adoption is strongly recommended by the RFU. There are five primary signals given to indicate the following: a try, penalty, free-kick, scrum and advantage. With the exception of advantage the referee would have stopped the game by blowing his whistle and then using one of the five signals to indicate who will restart the game and how. For penalty-kicks and free-kicks the better referees will signal clearly and quickly so that the non- offending team can take advantage by taking the kick quickly if they wish. The advantage signal is the only signal that is not preceded with a whistle. This is used when the referee spots an infringement, but chooses not to stop the game as the non-offending team have an opportunity to gain an advantage by playing on.

Secondary signals usually follow primary signals and are used to explain the reason for making an award to one side or the other. Referees are encouraged to adopt the use of secondary signals, but they are not compulsory. Perhaps a couple of examples would best demonstrate the correct procedure:

A) Referee spots a knock-on from which the non-offending team can gain no advantage.

1) He blows his whistle to stop play.
2) He moves to the place where the knock-on occurred
3) He gives the primary signal for a scrum (outstretched arm parallel to the ground pointing to the side with the right to put the ball in).
4) He gives the secondary signal for a knock-on (one hand above the head tapped by the other hand)

B) Referee spots a hooker winning the ball unfairly by having his boot raised before the ball enters the scrum.

1) He blows his whistle to stop play
2) He gives the primary signal for a free-kick (upper arm horizontal, forearm raised vertically pointing in the direction of the non-offending side)
3) He gives the secondary signal for boot-up (foot raised and heel tapped by hand).

In this way the players and spectators should all know why the game was stopped as well as how, where and by whom it is to be restarted.

Basically the Primary signals are used by the referee to indicate who has been awarded a try, scrum, free-kick, penalty, or advantage and the Secondary signals follow to explain why the awards were given.

It should be stressed that the use of signals is not compulsory, and many referees choose not to use all of t hem. The referees priority will be to get the decision right, and then to ensure that the players know what he has decided. This he might do by talking to them. If the explanation is accompanied by the appropriate signal, this is a bonus that is probably more appreciated by the isolated players such as the full-back, and the spectators.

There are many referees who do not agree with the signal for advantage being used. They would argue that for a side to know that a failure to gain an advantage will still result in a penalty kick, acts as an inducement to be more adventurous than they would have been otherwise.

16 OF THE MORE COMMON SIGNALS

Penalty kick *Shoulders parallel with touch line. Arm angled up, pointing towards non-offending team.*

Free kick *Shoulders parallel with touch line. Arm bent square at elbow, upper arm pointing towards non-offending team.*

Try and penalty try *Referee's back to dead-ball line. Shoulders parallel with goal line. Arm raised vertically.*

Advantage *Arm outstretched, waist high, towards non-offending team.*

Scrum awarded *Shoulders parallel with touch line. Arm horizontal, pointing towards team to put in the ball.*

Knock-on *Hands at level of head. Fingers of one hand tap the palm of the other hand.*

Not releasing ball immediately *Both hands are close to the chest, as if holding an imaginary ball.*

Diving to ground near tackle *Straight-arm gesture, pointing downwards to imitate diving action.*

Prop pulling down opponent *Clenched fist, and arm bent. Gesture imitates pulling opponent down.*

Foot-up by front-row player *Foot raised, heel touched.*

Handling ball in ruck or scrum *Hand at ground level, making sweeping action, as if handling the ball.*

Barging in line-out *Arm horizontal, elbow pointing out. Arm and shoulder move outwards as if barging opponent.*

Pushing opponent in line-out *Both hands at shoulder level, with palms outward, making pushing gesture.*

Lifting player in line-out *Both fists clenched in front, at waist level, making lifting gesture.*

Obstruction in general play *Arms crossed in front of chest at right angles to each other, like open scissors.*

High tackle (foul play) *Hand moves horizontally in front of neck.*

RED AND YELLOW CARDS

For matters of discipline the RFU delegates its authority to the constituent bodies of which there are 32 in England. Each of these constituent bodies must provide a disciplinary committee, who have the power to expel, or inflict other appropriate punishment, to any club or individual infringing the laws of the game. Our local constituent body is the Leicestershire Rugby Football Union, and they have a disciplinary committee made up of a chairman, secretary and 8 panel members. The panel members come from representatives of clubs who play within the county and a minimum of 4 must be present to form the committee. A member of the Leicestershire Society of Rugby Union Referees is also invited to attend every disciplinary committee meeting, but with the possible exception of being asked for guidance on a particular point of law, he is there solely for the purpose of observing in order to report back to the Society.

Following the ordering-off of a player the referee should write a report and send copies to his own Society, the constituent body where the game was played and the constituent body of the player's team (these might be the same). This should be done within 48 hours. It is then the responsibility of the constituent body where the game was played to organise a disciplinary hearing within 14 days. The player who was ordered-off should take no further part in training or playing rugby football, until after this hearing. The referee and the player ordered off are invited to attend and the player may also bring a club representative and other witnesses.

The proceedings within the hearing are quite formal starting with the reading of the referee's report followed by the player's statement. Although witnesses can be called in, any further evidence can only be put forward in clarification of the referee's report. The disciplinary committee are obliged to follow the letter of the law which states "The referee is the sole judge of fact and of law". A club official can speak up as a character reference for the player after which all parties are asked to leave the room while the committee members make their decision. If guilty, the player is asked to pay the administration costs of the meeting and given a sentence in accordance to RFU guidelines.

The introduction of a new soccer style card system this season has proved to be quite controversial (especially in Leicester). Remembering that law 26 (foul play) has not changed and that most referees can recognise a sending off offence when they see one, I do not think that many people would object to the use of the red card, which makes it very clear to all what is going on – or should I say off? Even the showing of a yellow card to make it clear that the player is being officially cautioned for misconduct and a dismissal for two yellow cards in one game would be in line with last season and acceptable. The controversy is being caused by the totting up of yellow cards from one game to another.

A player shown two yellow cards in any one season even if the games are 30 weeks apart is deemed to have been ordered off. The only difference between receiving a red card or two yellow cards in separate games is that the red card offender must stop training and playing rugby immediately, where as the two yellow card offender may continue to train and play until his hearing.

When in Leicester on 10th October, the National Referee Development Officer, Steve Griffiths, was asked if he could give any feed-back on how the card system was going and he replied that all of the top referees were in favour of it! What do you think?

DISCIPLINE

The article above was published in the Leicester Tigers programme on 28th October 1995. Six months later it appeared that Steve Griffiths had a change of mind, as the following is an extract from the National Referees Development Officer's March 1996 monthly update:

"Because of the totting process, the use of the YELLOW CARDS for general warnings has caused some unforeseen confusion. Please do not use Yellow Cards for general warnings, but explain to the captain of the offending team that if his team offends again a player will be sent from the field of play, or in the case of persistent infringement you will issue a Yellow Card to the next offender and a Red Card to the offender after that."

This instruction will now have been seen by every active referee in England, and should result in a more miserly distribution of yellow cards throughout the first five divisions. Yellow and red cards are not used for games in lower divisions.

Further to this action, the RFU have circulated a proforma to all 'A' list referees and senior clubs, asking for their opinion on the card system, and the season's experiment with the totting-up process.

DISCIPLINE UPDATE

A New Law Bulletin for the 1996/97 season states that there will be a National Disciplinary Committee to cover clubs in Courage Leagues 1 to 3, and there will be no totting-up process operating for yellow cards. (Steve Griffiths must have read my article.) The Bulletin also states that the red and yellow card system would be extended to cover all games at all levels, from the beginning of the 1996/97 season.

Following a case resulting in the imprisonment of a player, the RFU have advised referees to consider the ordering off of a player as a first resort. Many referees in the past have felt that they should try and keep players on the field, and only ordered them off as a last resort.

New procedures have also been implemented changing what might happen to a player after he has been ordered off. The mandatory suspension which prevented a player taking part in games up to his disciplinary hearing has been abolished. It was thought that in some cases, having to leave the field may be sufficient punishment. This does not stop the clubs from suspending their own player, following an ordering off. The clubs can now take more responsibility in this area, and actions they take will be taken into consideration by the disciplinary committee.

Players are still allowed to appeal against any penalty they get, but have to pay a fee in advance, which would not be returned if they were unsuccessful. This has been introduced to deter frivolous appeals.

For players under the age of 17 years, cases should be dealt with by the club, and the action taken is to be reported to the constitutional body.

The recommended penalty suspensions for foul play are:
- Punching – 30 days
- Kicking or raking – 60 days
- Unfair use of a boot – 60 days
- Head butting or assault – 60 days
- Abuse of match official – 120 days
- Striking match official – ban for life

EVOLUTION OF THE REFEREE

The present law book states that "During a match the referee is the sole judge of fact and of law," but this has not always been the case.

Until the year 1896, the two captains decided whether the game should be stopped or allowed to continue. Such a system, dependant solely on the goodwill of the two captains had its problems – slow to administer and open to dispute – and in 1885 the RFU laid down that two umpires and a referee be appointed to control the game. These officials however, could only adjudicate, the captains of the teams still had, as in cricket, to appeal for a decision. Ironically, it was this system which produced the law – that of advantage – which most distinguishes rugby football, for no captain would appeal for a stoppage if his team had gained an advantage from his opponent's mistake.

By 1889, the umpires had become touch judges, and by 1896 the practice of appeals was done away with, and the phrase "The referee shall be the sole judge of fact" was inserted in the Laws.

Today's referee continues to apply the principle of advantage, established so long ago by not whistling for an infringement which gives an advantage to the non-offending team. This is the law that sets rugby football aside from all other ball games, and it is the application of this law which distinguishes a good referee from a poor one. The better referees should approach the game looking for reasons NOT to blow their whistle. Will somebody tell them!

FIT TO REF?

There has been much discussion on what makes a good referee. In my opinion, and in the simplest of terms, I believe that the better referees are consistent, fair and good 'man managers', who have a good knowledge of the law and are fit enough to get themselves in the correct position to apply it.

Fitness has become more crucial in the past two seasons, since the law-makers have made every effort to keep the game faster and more free flowing.

In its efforts to keep the ball 'alive' the law makes it very clear what the tackler or tackled player may, or may not do whilst on the floor. It is also very clear what the supporting players may or may not do, when approaching a tackle situation. The highest standards are essential when refereeing these specific laws if the game is to develop into the fast, free flowing game desired by all. In order to achieve this, today's referee must be capable of getting to every breakdown as soon as, if not before, the supporting players. That is to say the modern referee should be covering the field in his particular standard of game, at the same rate as the open side flankers. When a referee is ten or fifteen yards away from a breakdown, it is obviously more difficult for him to see what is happening, but even if from this distance he is able to pick out the FIRST OFFENDER, he will find that being those extra few yards off the pace of the game, will severely erode his credibility among the players.

This is recognised by the RFU and all senior referees are obliged to take a fitness test twice each season and failure to achieve the required standard would mean automatic downgrading.

THE TOUCH JUDGE

For years the job of running the line was done by an injured player, an elder-statesman of the club, or even by a lone spectator who foolishly showed up before the kick-off time. In the early seventies, when I was playing for Leicester the touch was always run by the club coach, Chalkie White.

When the league structure was introduced in 1987, the Senior clubs were very quick to complain about the standard of touch judging, and although they all believed that their own touch judges were perfectly fair and competent, they did not feel the same way about the touch judges provided by their opponents. This led to the introduction of RFU appointed touch judges for all games at divisions 4 and above. Nowadays the officials are very much a team of three, trained to work together with the referee as the leader.

Before each game the touch-judges are briefed by the referee, who explains his requirements of them. Their most obvious priority is to judge if the ball is in touch, but there are now numerous other ways in which they are expected to assist the referee. The senior touch judge often briefs the ball boys, who must not touch a ball that could be used for a quick throw, nor should they give a spare ball directly to a player, as in this instance it should be placed by the ball boy on the line of touch. When the ball has gone into touch the touch judge should raise his flag and run to the line of touch but should not raise his other arm to indicate who's throw-in it is until after the right to take a quick throw has gone (when a line out is formed, or the ball touched by a spectator). In this way the referee gains additional information, helping him to judge if a quick throw is legal or not.

Generally throughout the game the three officials attempt to "triangulate" on the ball. For instance if the ball emerging from a scrum is moved towards touch judge 'A' he will lead and run along his line ahead of the ball. Touch judge 'B' should dwell level with the place the scrum took place long enough to ensure that all players are proceeding to the next play and not indulging in illegal activities. The referee who makes up the third point of the triangle will keep close to the ball. This trangulation is shown in the diagrams opposite.

Various other aids are offered for the assistance of the referee, such as marking the off-side line for the side not in possession at line-outs and penalty kicks etc., and indicating whether a try has been scored in a difficult corner-flag situation. These qualified touch judges are also instructed to signal misconduct and foul play, by raising their flag parallel to the ground and pointing across the pitch. If this is done the referee will stop the game while the touch judge reports a player, the offence and his recommended action. The RFU are very keen on the concept of the officials working as teams of three, and over recent seasons various experiments have been conducted where the referee was wired up to his touch judges for sound (see page 55).

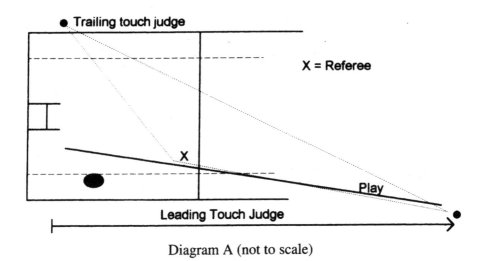

Diagram A (not to scale)

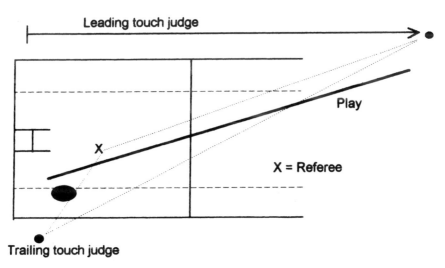

Diagram B (not to scale)

TIME KEEPING

The referee is the sole judge of time, although I expect it will not be long before the likes of Murdoch and Packer will be dictating when matches should start, finish and how many 'time-outs' there should be to allow for advertisements.

Presently the game consists of two halves of forty minutes duration, with a break for half-time to allow the players to change ends and prepare for the second half. The referee can allow up to five minutes for half-time, but in effect the players are usually ready to continue well within the time allotted. Once the game has started the referee should add on time for delays in the half of the match in which the delay occurs. To assist in accurate timing, most referees use a stop-watch, backed up by a second time-piece.

When a player is injured the referee can allow a stoppage of up to one minute for treatment, unless a longer period is necessary to remove the player, or to give essential treatment on the playing area. He should not allow time if he believes that a player is feigning injury. When the ball is dead, time can be allowed for a player to replace or repair a torn jersey or shorts, but no time should be allowed for a player to re-tie or repair a bootlace – I don't know why, as a loose bootlace, in my opinion, is a hazard that could cause a player to trip and injure himself; however the law is quite specific on this matter.

Some of the longest delays (and often the most blatant time-wasting) occur when a player takes the option of kicking at goal. Referees are instructed to add on any time taken in excess of 40 seconds from the time the player indicates his intention to kick at goal. This applies whether or not the referee considers the delay to be 'undue delay' on the part of the kicker.

When a period of forty minutes has expired the referee can only blow for time when the ball is dead. However, if the ball next becomes dead as a result of one team scoring a try, that team should be allowed to take the conversion kick and if the ball becomes dead as a result of a fair catch, free-kick or penalty kick the game should continue. As there is no limit to the number of penalties or free kicks that a referee can award after forty minutes has expired, the game can often be extended for a considerable length of time.

The referee does have the power to declare no-side before time has expired, if in his opinion the full time cannot be played, or the continuance of play would be dangerous. If a league game is stopped because of weather conditions the time of the abandonment becomes crucial. If more than 60 minutes of rugby has been played then the score at the time of abandonment becomes the match result, and if less than 60 minutes is played the two teams should play again within seven days. The outcome of a game that is stopped for any reason other than weather conditions will be determined by the organising committee of the league concerned.

During the 1995/96 seasons the RFU introduced official timekeepers for first division games, and they assumed sole responsibility for the time keeping of each game. Sitting at the side of the pitch they run a stop watch (starting and stopping it at the appropriate times) and blow a loud hooter to end each half.

SOUND CONNECTIONS

The RFU have been experimenting with the use of two-way radio links between the referee and touch-judges since 1993. Such tests were introduced because it was thought that off-side was becoming prevalent and beginning to stifle the game. Also, as the games were getting faster it was becoming an impossible task for one official to police the off-side laws in all circumstances. Eventually modern technology has produced a system that is generally thought to be simple to use, robust, unobtrusive, with completely clear two-way sound reception. This system has been in use for all first division games since March 1996, and will continue to be used in the future.

Having found a suitable system, the RFU have given the referees and touch-judges clear guidelines as to how it should be used. Touch-judges are aware that a 'running commentary on the game' is not what is required, and they should use the system rarely but positively. Any information they choose to give to the referee is exactly that – and not a signal for action. The referee remains the sole judge of fact and of the law. The main objectives are to keep the players on-side, giving the team in possession their legal space in which to work, and to eliminate foul play.

When using the system, some referees have found that they were not expecting communication, and not being ready for it, they missed the first few words. Also some found their concentration shifting from the game to the communication. Clearly much practice is required before all of the senior officials will be able to maximise on the obvious advantages of two-way communication.

On all occasions when the officials are connected for sound, the players have been informed before the kick-off. This in itself has been a deterrent, in a similar way to the 'cardboard cut-out policemen' used on the motorway. Players at the highest level are now aware that any attempt to cheat, behind the referee's back, will probably be reported by the touch-judge, and result in a penalty against the team. Feedback tells us that players are enjoying the additional space created by the use of the system, when they are the side in possession, and they find it acceptable provided it is used fairly and consistently.

The radio equipment has been purchased by the RFU, and sent to each of the first-division clubs, where it becomes the responsibility of the newly appointed Referee Co-ordinators. These officers are generally responsible for the management and control of communications and hospitality arrangements for referees, touch-judges, referee advisors, referee coaches, and time-keepers who are appointed to officiate at their club. Since the introduction of the communication system, it is the responsibility of these officers to see that the radio equipment is fully charged and available on the day of the match, along with the stop watch and klaxon for the official time-keeper.

How far are we from having a second referee in the stand, with a play-back screen, as seen in Cricket and American Football?

ABOUT THE AUTHOR

Growing up in Devon with an enthusiasm for a wide range of sports, Mike Mortimer discovered rugby at St. John's Teacher Training College, York. Beginning as a wing threequarter, in his second season he moved to the second row, found the position suited him well, and other sports took a back seat.

In 1965 he moved to Leicestershire to teach, with his sights set on a place in the Leicester Tigers team, but in the meantime introduced the Martin High School, Anstey, to rugby. Within three years the school was able to field teams at all age levels, as it still does.

In his personal ambitions Mike found that at 6ft 2in he was deemed too small for a top-level second-row forward, so turned to local club rugby. But after four years, he made another attempt for the Tigers, this time as a tight-head prop. Following some difficult moments in his first matches, Mike established himself as the first choice for this position in 1971, and over the next five seasons made 132 first team appearances, as well as being selected for Leicestershire, Devon, and Midland Counties.

Retiring from the first-class game in 1976, he returned to his local club – Stoneygate – where he continued to play for a further six seasons – as club captain for two of them. By 1982, beginning to feel the knocks, Mike changed tack, and joined the surprisingly competitive world of refereeing, through the Leicestershire Society of Referees. In his search for progress in his new pastime, Mike identified two potential weaknesses. Firstly, despite years of playing rugby, he became aware how limited was his knowledge of the laws of the game, and secondly, by now he was forty years old. To overcome the first problem, he religiously studied one law each day, repeatedly over a two year period, to gain the depth of understanding he required. He is still searching for a solution to the second, which is now bordering on the chronic.

However, his rise through the ranks was rapid, and within three years had made the Midland Counties 'B1' list, revisiting as referee the grounds around the country that he had previously been to as a player. After twelve years of refereeing senior rugby, Mike retired and returned to the Leicester Tigers as a selector, as well as a contributor to the club programme.

Along with these jobs Mike has taken on the newly created post of Referee Coordinator – responsible for management and hospitality arrangements for referees, touch judges, assessors and time keepers at home games.

He remains a full member of the Leicestershire Society of Referees, where he was elected chairman for seven years, and is currently the Training Officer. On Sunday mornings he can still be seen out and about in the Leicestershire clubs, refereeing junior rugby.